Ophelia

ACKNOWLEDGEMENTS

Acknowledgements are due to the editors of *Chapman, Inter Arts, Lines Review, New Poetry II* (Quartet, 1988), *A Touch of Flame* (Lion, 1989), *Original Prints III* (Polygon, 1989) and *Twenty of the Best* (Galliard, 1990), where some of these poems first appeared.

Ophelia
and other poems

Elizabeth Burns

Polygon
EDINBURGH

© Elizabeth Burns 1991

Polygon
22 George Square, Edinburgh

Set in Linotron Sabon
by Koinonia, Bury, and
printed and bound in
Great Britain by
Redwood Press,
Melksham, Wiltshire

British Library Cataloguing in
    Publication Data
Burns, Elizabeth
    Ophelia and other poems
    I. Title
    821'.914

ISBN 0 7486 6096 8

The publisher acknowledges subsidy from
the Scottish Arts Council
towards the publication of this volume.

CONTENTS

SISTERS

Even when she moved
five hundred miles away
telepathy was alive between them
and love as strong as ever

She sends in the post
pressed tulip petals
slivers of shell from the day at the beach
wrapped in tissue paper

She, a book of stories
golden earrings

and she, the painting of a windy day
the daffodil bowl

Even before the letter
saying, between the lines, 'come',
she is on her way

MERIDIAN

Climbing Observatory Hill
we see Greenwich like an old engraving
mapped out below:
trim, white and elegant
shipping office, naval college
and Cutty Sark's rigging
spiking the sky

Here at the top of the hill
the meridian
is a short mark in concrete
where the world is split
into east and west

Here time is determined
by the absolute accuracy
of the clock
and on the dot
of one o'clock
the ball drops
from the tower
time is checked
and the watchers
feel precise
and grounded
by the correct
mean time

But tomorrow
you will go to another hemisphere
gaining a dayful of hours
that do not exist
and at one o'clock
in the afternoon
when the sign is made
from the Greenwich tower
you will be sleeping
under a southern moon
and east and west will begin
from the line of where you lie
dreaming, a meridian

THE OPIUM OF POETRY

The pipe is long and elegant –
De Quincey fingers it
admires the ivory
passes it to Coleridge
whose eyes fix on the golden birds
which in his mind
are flying out to sea
through an ivory sky
over an empty ship –
smoke is floating from it –
he breathes it now
so thick and choking sweet
and Wordsworth is leaning
towards him and
lifting the pipe
tasting its metal in his mouth
touching its tiny carvings –
little Chinese bridges
rivers, houses, gardens –
and imagining the people
who live in the bamboo houses
with poppies in their gardens
who cook on fires
that are catching the houses alight –
there is a strange smell of burning –
it is the poppies –
they are flaming
and he is passing the pipe
back to De Quincey
who has a pen in one hand

and is dipping it in ink
and beginning to write
as poetry wafts
like heady smoke
through Dove Cottage –

and I am sitting
a pen in my hand
and the opium pipe beside me
and Wordsworth, Coleridge, De Quincey
(and Carlyle, found today in a skip)
are on the shelves of Colin's room
where poetry is in the air
and we're writing in a circle
that is complete now
because Thelma's back
from visiting Wordsworth's house
and Carlyle's birthplace

and I have walked here
along the street where De Quincey stayed
past the house where Caroline lives
now that she's left her job
at Dove Cottage, and come here
with the exhibition on De Quincey

and we are gathered round this fire
passing objects to make poems from
I pass the opium pipe to Chris –
it is long and elegant
he fingers it
admires the ivory
passes it on –

GOING BACK TO CHAPELTON

July, barefoot, she is running outside
for breathfuls of the clean breezy air that ruffles
the sycamore, brushes the fur of the barley
while the valley full of pastel fields
is lit by the passing of pale sun
that drifts through clouds to Dunsinane.

Here at the border between garden and farm
they plant out little cabbages
opal leaves flopping onto black soil
and unearth yellowed pebbles of potatoes
and carrots, wrinkled and minute as babies' fingers.
Witchlike, she slices them in with the peas

startled emerald and sweet from their pods
then there are bowlfuls of scarlet strawberries
unwashed, earthy, rough against the tongue
until teeth bite the slice of pink.
They eat them by the crackle of the applewood fire
summer and winter jarring together

and she is dreaming back to how it was before
snow feet-deep around the cottage
iced air frosting your throat as you breathed
and how that evening they talked and drank
in the close circle of the fire, fed flames
that glanced on flagons of elderflower wine

and so covered by the snow of love were they,
thinking its blanket of beauty and oblivion
would never melt as they held close
to warm flesh and woke entwined
to sun skimming through iced glass,
that they never dreamt of passion's thaw.

Mellowed summer is gentle:
marigolds at the door, a nestling of herbs
rosemary, erica, borage, sage
lupins seeded and raspberries become
plump rows of ripe fruit
where then they were bare canes stalking the snow.

But she wishes not for this slack fecund laziness
of summer months with no needlepoint sharpness
to the light, but remembers and weeps for
the weight and delight of snow
its sheer icing and the stabs at the heart
of stalactite.

SAINT CATHERINE'S MONASTERY

It is a place of bones.

Catherine's herself lie safely fleshless
shrined in a blue box in her own chapel.

Martyred in the desert, a monastery
grew round her skeleton, dry bones
sprouting a place of pilgrimage
a place of cypresses and olives
green in the wafer-dry peninsula
that holds out its thirsty tongue
to lap the salt of the Red Sea.

For a thousand years monks have been here:
Greek-speaking, black-clad
drawn by some divining rod of vocation
to this source of water in the desert.

In this whitewashed room are heaped
the skulls of a millennium of them:
lining the walls, filling the cupboards
lying in mounds on the floor
each one exhumed and here exhibited
anonymous, having lost below earth
that skin that was the colour of rock at sunrise
and the eye brown as a fresh date
the black ringlet threaded with a silk of white hair
the crinkle which the smile carved.

It is a place where bones are casually shown
where they have become as normal
as the scant rockiness of landscape
that is all the eye has to look upon.

It is the monastery's grapefruit tree
it is the fact of pilgrims still arriving
or of one of the monks
offering cups of sweet tea
and biscuits flavoured with herbs
which in this strip of earth
is rarity, is miracle.

THE TAMARISK PICKERS

Driving through Sinai at dusk
the sun behind some mountain
the rocks becoming colourless

we come upon these women
crouched by the roadside
with their bulky bundles of leaves

There is a scrabble of Arabic
then they clamber in over rucksacks
We are eleven now in the taxi

It lurches and is heavy
with the thick musk of tamarisk
clinging to clothes and fingers

The faces of the women
are creviced like rock
Against them glint earrings

of hammered silver
and beneath black cloaks
are glimmerings of scarlet

At nightfall we reach the road-end
The women stumble out into darkness
wind lifting their cloaks like wings

In the morning they will return
for the bundles they left by the roadside
breathing tamarisk into the desert air

16

GOLD OF THE PHARAOHS: ITS DISCOVERY

An archaeologist penetrates the tomb

A dry desert place, this
a land cracked by salt, infertile

He comes into her, will take that
dry-legged bitch, open her cave

up – says she's barren, does she?
See what he can bring out of her

Look at the golden sons
he can make her give birth to

She wasn't barren after all
just needed someone like him

inside her
to make them all come spilling out

his golden sons, he'll take them off
to show around the world

While she lies empty, sterile, her womb
scraped out as bare as any other in this

sandblown childless place
of tombs and bones

and salty weepings for the time
when there were treasures here

VALDA'S POEM / SLEEVENOTES

Sleevenotes to Hugh MacDiarmid's record
Whaur Extremes Meet:
'Recorded at Brownbank, the home of
Valda and Chris Grieve, near Biggar in the
Lanarkshire hills on two sultry days in June
1978. Chris, in his chair by the window,
talking with his friend, the poet Norman
MacCaig, a wee dram in every glass. Valda
in swimsuit, working in the garden, or
keeping the soft-coated Wheaten and
Border Terrier quiet for the recording.'

June sun presses on my back as I bend
sweat gathers at my neck and under my arms
I am naked as I can be in my bathing costume

I step out onto the flowerbeds
making light footprints with my bare feet
Spray trails from the watering-can
falls in dark circles round the plants

I want to lie out on the parched grass
and let the sun's hands touch me everywhere
let them finger the frail flesh of my breasts
rub gold into the crease and wrinkle of my stomach

At the open window edged with ivy
they sit, two old men in their shirt-sleeves
On the table between them a bottle of whisky
the two fat volumes of collected poems
and a tape-recorder lapping up their words

The dog flops in the shade of the back door
I go to her when she stirs, stroke her hot fur
give her water, keep her from barking

I hear their talk and laughter, his and Norman's
I hear the rise and fall of Chris's voice
the rhythms of his favourite poems, over and over

In the afternoon I sit against the apple tree
feeling the dent of bark on my bare shoulders
I close my eyes and the murmur of their voices
blurs with the birdsong that maybe
when we listen to the finished record
will have swum inside the poems

MOTHER AND CHILD IN THE BOTANIC GARDENS

Baby carriages are not allowed in the plant houses

The baby floats carriage-less
in her waterlily cradle
that wafts and drifts her round the world

Australasia   Guatemala   Mexico
South Laos   Norfolk Islands   Crete

Wrapped in a coir of coconut
she floats from island to island

A bush with waxy orange flowers
bends between her and the sun
Purple berries fall into her lap
She eats them
and lays her head in the creamy pillow
of a lily flower

She is lost in Tropics of the Old World
Her dreams are scented

The mother comes running through the plant houses
tropical to temperate and back to tropical
frantic between the arms of palm trees
and the tangle of passion flowers
that curl their tendrils into her hair

Fronds of fern tickle and grip
Green surrounds her, a mouth of green is
eating her with jade lips
and a moist and mossy tongue
that licks her with a limey liquid
Cacti crawl at her feet
leer from their gravel and sand
claw their spikes and prickles into her skirts

and the iron skeleton
buckles and caves
Its bony fingers
waver in the lily pond

She looks into
its ochre water
and sees
curled on the deck
of a waterlily leaf
her daughter

her eyes gazing up to the glass roof
and her lips
stained with purple

JESUS SPEAKS TO THE CHURCH AT EASTERTIME

I have plans for you
you snoozer
you drowsy sluggish church

I resurrect myself
am off that cross
knowing what torture is:

your hand's palm (place where
sparrow, flax-flower
wheat-chaff were cupped)

has nails hit through it
cartilage crumbles like biscuit
body gapes, blood crusts

I get my limbs out
of those bloodied ribbons
musky gravecloths

step out past boulder and soldiers
into wet grass
Morning in a garden

Breakfast on a beach
Fingers falter at scabbed skin
touch, touch

I shake you like a mother at dawn
trying to wake a child
who flops like a rag doll

You doze and will not look
at daylight
Your dreams are easier

I resurrect
You eat chocolate eggs
sugary and melting

You mix me in with spring:
hatched birds, daffodils
all gaudy yellow things

never thinking of the southern hemisphere
where it is not spring
never looking at the church at the tip of Africa

It does not need posies, ribbons, baby rabbits
It has tasted crucifixion
real as nails or tear-gas

Its gold and green
are not the colours of primroses
but of freedom, potent

But here you lie in bed, snug and indulged
You do not see there is a day outside
and people living in it

Oh wilted church, what rags of hymns you sing
what mumbled scraps of prayers you speak
on the narrow track to your imagined heaven

Oh gaunt church, gaunt people
so silent and not dancing
not screaming

COLONIZERS

The colonizers came
to the island
dis-regarding it
desiring it

They will take the coconut
eat the mangoes
rape the women
reap the date palms

They will plant this land
with sugar-cane
and the people will work it for them
chained

The Carib ones
seeing them come
throw themselves
off the cliffs

rather their bones
be in the salt hands of the sea
than the scarring ones
of the slave-driver

and now none but the sea
mourns them
washing the shores of the island
with waves of grief

The colonizers came
to the island
dis-regarding it
desiring it

They will take the hills and glens
burn the houses
rape the women
trample the crofts

They will populate this land
with sheep
and the people will leave it for them
cleared

The Highland ones
evicted
take themselves
off in ships

driven out
upon the mercy of the sea
and the desolation
of exile

and now none but the sea
mourns them
washing the shores of the island
with waves of grief

REASON AND EMOTION

It is cool and stately here
It has porticoes and pillars
It is vast and white and well-lit
The paintings are suitably placed

Here we will examine
rationality
and see how these paintings
show the influence
of classicism
Note how we use its images
the toga for example
or the temple wall
Note how the buildings and the plants
are full of phalluses
and how we use a cast of Venus
as a symbol of beauty
and see how in this example
she has a silk thread
a red cut
about her throat

See how we represent order
with the straight lines
of our careful draughtsmanship
our abstract geometry
See how order represents
the civilised values
of a classical society
where men in formal gardens

discussed philosophy
while slaves made perfect buildings
according to directions

just as our assistants
now make works of art
while we drink wine
discuss aesthetic theory

But her dreams come at her crazily
and all the images of blood spill out
from the raw heart, the broken pillar
and its liquid drips onto the sand
while in the sky the lightning crackles
rises up in front of the cracked temple
and pulls at the river, making it rise and fall
lifting the sails of the bronze-carved barques
laden with wheat and led by leopards
Death and silty water, kohl around the eyes,
dreams of smearing the temple floor
breaking chunks of marble from the pillars
dreams of goddesses and rituals and an island
full of women

Emotion splatters messily
in this corner of the gallery
where something is
awry
and breathing

FALLING IN

falling from cliff into ocean a gust lifts you
holds you in air fleet seconds as your mind
gasps at the lush sea mouth and your scared eyes
skim the known grass, cling to clouds before the
fall and splash that gulps you with a green breath
laps you with the milk-searching tongues of waves
on wet flesh as your eyes open underwater
to a place of glassiness and you float salt-borne
between fish-glint and rings set with limpet
on the intricate fingers of coral and the emerald
banners of seaweed windlessly streaming

and now the seaworld holds you close
lures you with its swell and the daily pull of the moon
kisses you swift and silver, licks your skin
floods you with flash and dapple of fallen light
gathers you in endless folds of ocean's cliffless arms

DRIVING DOWN THE M1 THROUGH
WARWICKSHIRE

It's dusk in Shakespeare's country, wet June
and hard to slit the sky's cloak, drooped grey cloth
over squelchy earth that snugs the bones of those
who lived within a tiny tightened world
that reached its arms from Orton water or
the Avon; beyond that, only rumours
blown on grass seeds, telling the city's fables
grown queer, enormous, in repeating.

How would the skin wrinkle on these skeletons
and the eyes, were they to see, become aghast
at the strap of motorway slapped down
over the place of graves, searing oak woods,
scurrying with car and lorry monsters
that gulp the leagues to London in the time
it once took to walk to the market and back;

or the trousered women, truck driving,
sucking from a parchment box the sweet thick
juice of a spiky fruit called pineapple
nibbling pastries from a place named India;
or the inns at the roadside as high as
cathedrals, but plain-glass windowed, spireless.

Dusk, but Shakespeare's country, and his words have
sown cornfields, heaped harvest in granaries,
give breath to the fluttering heart of the past.

AUTUMN IN THE GRAVEYARD

In blurry reds and purples (colours of musty hymnbooks)
berries, wet with melted frost, emerge from spiky briars,
spurt out, at a tooth's bite, a sweet blood
to be boiled, fermented, into jam or wine, or simply
taken warm upon the kissed tongue.

Fruits' stalks scratch marble, clamber lichened crosses
stained with seeped juice, and with the faint, glinting
thin as spiders' webs, gold trails, filigrees:
symbols of women, drawings of the moon
that weave fine threads through damp leaves, add gleam
to rampant fruit that shrouds the smudged engravings
and devours the angels made of stone.

UNTITLED LOVE POEM

to give words to what has been   and what you are
is   in the face of feckless language   impossible
words are such skimpy   scrawly creatures   such
scant indications   of immensities   and depths
that trying for   definition   or for poetry
I'm left with   slippery abstracts   piling up
as far from what I want to say   as printed ovals
are from music   when it gets out into the air
paltry   vocabulary   fails me
scratches on a surface   mere hieroglyphics
but beyond this   in a sturdy   wordless
place   of glance and touch   I will lay out
offerings of   vast   unwritten gifts

IN AN ATTIC ROOM

a mothy flutter of gaslight
shafts soft yellow
on worn wood of floor and chair
glimmers the white porcelain
of waterless washstand
with its shell-shaped soap places
falls on the jar of pink roses
makes shadows in the folds
below each petal

turn off the lamp and the mantle glows
fading from light to darkness
from hiss of gas to silence

those who are lying
curved in the soft bed
like shells in sand
touch in the quiet dark
knowing exactly the feel
of a finger's tracing
the place of flesh
the brush of eyelash on face

through the glass of skylight
the night of midsummer is a blur of mauve

at dawn it lifts to milky grey
makes visible the shadowed shapes
of kist, basket, candlestick
the colours in the patchwork

and in the drift between dark and daylight
there are kisses in half sleep
before the eyes are opened

before they look to the place
where the island lies
a ghost of itself
sifted over with mist

but shaped by punch of glaciers and gales
shove and shunt of moon on waves
the grindings and shiftings of sand

this frail and almost mirage island
is rock

SOUTH AMERICA : DREAMS AND FEARS

I

I almost committed suicide

said the woman balanced on the rock
with the waves of the Pacific crashing round her

said the woman balanced on the rock
with the waves of the Atlantic crashing round her

so easy to fling myself down through the fathoms
to the soft and sandy seabed

but I clung like a mermaid
to my rock on the coast of Chile

but I clung like a mermaid
to my rock on the coast of Argentina

with the wild waves breaking round me
and here I am, alive

II

Freedom, said Marta, *was running and running*
along a beach until I collapsed from exhaustion

I was so weak from the prison
Around her neck she wears a stone her sister carved

while they were both in jail
under the junta

III

In the dream we are running, my sister and I
along a beach in Patagonia

thinking we have freedom now in the reach of our
        arms
in the stretch of this vast cartwheeling shore

where the waves are high as houses
so loud you could scream at them and not be heard

We have dropped the clothes our father lent us
left them lying on the rust-coloured sand

lit queerly by the light of an orange sun
the sea itself sepia, waves curling like milky coffee

But barbed wire keeps us from the ocean
We run on a dream sand and cannot get close

to the freedom we think we have found
A beach is only freedom

when you have known its opposite
and have ceased to be afraid

IV

In a dream about Neruda
he leaves a book of poems

a loaf of bread
a bunch of red carnations

gifts for his country
weathering the storms

V

I have cut barbed wire in the wet night
and been shunted off by boy-soldiers

I have had tear-gas in my face
and insults shouted at me

but I have avoided arrest
I have been afraid of cells

I have never tasted the nearness of death
either in threats or blunt at my throat

I still have the garments of my fathers
safely folded round me

I have not been naked yet
I have no stone around my neck

I give only crumbs of bread
crumpled petals of flowers

poems that will be
washed away by the sea

THE BURIAL GARDEN

The mourning of this death was a crazy grief
that swamped his mind with tears he could not cry

Then he conceived the plan of a memorial
a garden: very sparse and Japanese

He laid flat slabs of white and grey
over the straggling grass

He channelled water into a pool
let lilies float on it

Around this, little bluish pine trees
fresh-scented shrubs, white pebbles

a block of creamy sculpture
marked by curves of soft glazed blue

and at the edges of the garden blossom trees,
magnolias, a few narcissi

The garden lay serene as windless water
his mind floated calm as a lily

until, with the sadness faded,
new obsessions possessed him

and over the memorial garden
he grew extra grass for grazing

and now it is an eerie field
where sheep munch in the mornings

But below the green veneer
of lightly nibbled lawn

lie the bones of a garden
and at the dried pool's edge

where the ghost of water seeps
the grass is squelched and mossy

and beneath his mask of healing
is a skeleton of grief

and lying heavy on his cool dry mind
is all the liquid weight of unshed tears

A GIFT

You bring me two shells
from the bay of Talisker

I lick the salt of the sea from them
and keep them in my pocket

Fingering them
I think of two things

The beauty of the island
The delicacy of your love

OPHELIA

Still harping on daughters

Always the daughter
her movements round the castle
charted by her father

She has a wide-armed gangly innocence
she is motherless and milky
an innocent in the court
Her flesh is thin as manuscript
her eyes are animal and scared
Ribbons hang from her hair
her skirts are hitched up awkwardly
cling to her gawky legs
make her gauche among armour

Always the daughter

But Hamlet – he –
she licks the ink of his letters
fingers the string of pearls he gave her
that swing between her breasts
– he – but he is ungraspable

He will not talk to her as adult:
he confides in Horatio
walks off, untouchable, to man's talk
He basks in the words of Horatio:
the days are not long enough to listen to his wisdom
He wants it to be just the two of them together

plotting Denmark's future:
no women to distract them

He laughs now at the old love letters
he once wrote her, tosses them in the fire
He wants her gone
His words clang in her head:
Get thee to a nunnery

She is trapped in this tilted castle
and this man who has drawn such promises from her
who has given her gifts of pearls
spits in her eye and slaps her face:
his handmark makes a red flag
across her pale cheek

He will not listen, he will not
listen when she says she loves him,
love big as these pounding waves
that salt the windows
Every word she wrote and spoke was true
but Hamlet will not hear her

Each day she tiptoes on a slippery bank –
one step and she would over-edge from sanity
feeling rocks grown slithery with moss
slide from her grasp as whirlpool water looms

This is not the beautiful floating death by water
She will not have her skirts drawn out around her
billowed along by the current
her hair floating like some golden weed
and a cloak of wildflowers scattered round her

This death by water
will be sticky with mud
Her wet clothes will drag her down
and the stones in her pockets
sink her quickly

She reaches out to Hamlet
through filmy salt-spattered windows –
he drifts through her fingers
she cannot make herself heard –

Madness flows between them like a river
They say that his is faked
They say that hers is real

She gives herself over to flowers
and songs and bitter-scented herbs
rubbed and rubbed through her fingers

It is very hazy and blossomy here, and loud –
she cannot make herself heard
between the rantings of the courtiers

She is walled by this castle, she is liege
Her father's eyes are on her
The ramparts clutch at her –

she looks to shores of Elsinore
and sees the men set sail
for England, and for France

But she will float away

bedraggled down the stream –
water will take her
She has her pockets weighted
and her hair garlanded

She went down singing
so they say

Ophelia
Ophelia
Ophelia –

WORK AND ART / WE ARE BUILDING A
CIVILIZATION

Backs aching from carrying stones
Eyes blind from straining at needles
Toe-bones crushed
Fingers arthritic

Is Acropolis more marvellous
than silk embroidered sheets

because white marble in sun
because hill-top
because visible
because men?

Does quarrying of stone
hefting it up hillside
mean more magic
than picking of raw flax
spinning cotton through cut fingers?

Why in museums
are spacious airy rooms
given up to the bulging statues
of naked men
while all the little intricacies
the workings of gold
spiralled with shell-copied delicacy
are shoved on high shelves
cluttered and dusty
almost out of sight?

They will know us by what remains
what is preserved
and what restored

Cracks in a wall
Shreds in silk
The feast of acid rain
or moth

This stone-cleaning has sponsors
from all over the world
but who will mend
the worn cloth
the frayed embroidery?

It is more important
that we have a record of the olive-oil harvest
than that we know what the oracles once spoke

This is how we will be known
We are making our own history

We are preserving our relics
There is art
and folk art

and all the soft draped curtains
and embroidered folds of cloth
are become folk art

They do not lie in gold and crimson waves
on the steps of the Parthenon
They are locked away in labyrinths of backstreets

The blood from pricked fingers
splattered on white linen
is red as the poppy petals
scattered over the Acropolis

But it is the white glare of marble
that is fingered and stroked

not the skin-frail silk of poppies
that flare under moonlight
and every spring
converge in crevices
to flower again in scarlet
through the stonework

BECAUSE

Because she took the photo of her window-sill
with the blue-grey jug and the bowl of lemons
and because you found in a chest of drawers
the photograph of what was now your window-sill
your view, and made a painting of it for me
and I placed it opposite my bed,
I am sitting in this city looking out
through a painted window to a wet green field
with a wooden stile and high grasses
and above it a sky of creamy yellow
edging into a mist of blue, very pale
and on the window-sill is set a jug, a bowl of lemons

THE ODDITY

She is a crooked planet: does not fit
in the thin universe of this house
that peoples itself with gentlefolk
who blink as though they do not see her
when she asks to use the library.

There is a clanking housekeeper
whose spiked mouth, licked, would give off poison,
and a cluster of maidservants
who, in the mothballed linen cupboard,
will gossip on the newcomer.

It's whispered that she's delicate
is delivered of bowls of sopped bread
bland milk puddings
but Cook sees her, the little witch,
sneaking herbs from the kitchen garden.

This household's under the thumb
of the chimes of the grandfather clock
Nothing here is tainted by imagination's kiss
and nothing queer-eyed or peculiarly skinned
gets out to roam the corridors

so that she, with her silences and pencils
her barefoot tiptoeing over the flagstones
in her old grey muslin dress
that billows out in draughty stairwells
feels freak: hears laughter

frothing in the steamy kitchen
whispers bubbling under doors,
is trailed by soft footsteps, rustling silks,
but reaches the room: a fastness:
turns the brass key in the lock behind her.

Soon there will be apron-smothered giggles
outside her door: she will rise
stuff the keyhole with a handkerchief
to block the peering eyes
then draw the shades against the lilac sky

and in thin dusk-light, take ink,
begin, in copperplate,
though hot tears plop, and blot the page,
and voices batter at her head
like scatty moths, to write.

POEMS OF DEPARTURE

I

in the dream we are in New York   walking the
    humid streets
under an orange sunset   blurred with smog
but the houses seem too old and foreign   to belong
    here
we cannot find   5th avenue   east 12th street
and everywhere's too quiet and too beautiful for
    New York City

an old man with a horse and cart   shuffles past
along deserted gutters   selling white roses

it becomes in the dream   a city of the old world
of quaint houses   the scent of roses in the streets

Europe and America   split by an ocean   the two of us
wrenched between   the old world   and the new

II

I feel as a child about to be abandoned
who screams at her mother 'I don't love you anyway'
I have a stack of sharpened words inside me
that I pull out to wound you with
make little nicks in your skin
instead of kisses   but at the same time
I want to be curled in the crook of your arm
I want things like lullabies and cocoa
an abundance of tendernesses

III

of these last days together I will remember
the motherly holding of one another
the placing in my lap   of the grey and white shell
that you found on the beach at Ardalanish

and your calm voice reading poetry into the night
keeping sadness at bay   though how sibling close it
    creeps
until its breath is all over me   inside my imagination
making the tears come at my throat   a blue-grey
    sobbing

IV

fat globe   I want to punch you
batter away   at your enormity
I hate you for the   gaps you make
for your infinite   wildernesses
of continents   and oceans
you smug   plump   planet

V

I dream of infidelity   of a woman who discovers
her husband's unfaithfulness abroad
knots silk scarves together   into a noose
pulls it tight   around her neck

VI

we are living in a limbo   in a half life
in the almost colourless place   where the limp tongue
of the last of day   licks the sky with faint colours
slight flickers   of green or apricot
these are the shades   we live with
in the place between daylight   and darkness
in the place between your being here   and leaving

VII

the white candle of our last evening   still burns
the white flowered violet that you gave me   blossoms
light falls   on your gift of the rose garden painting

the room is ghosted   with your presence
and remembrances   pungent as rosemary
seep through   the muslin of the heart

AT PLATH'S GRAVE

Smoke-black Heptonstall
tight-lipped and cobbled
drawn nets, closed doors
curt and wind-beaten

She the freak, the poet
buried on this moor-top
where a harsh wind scrapes the sky
cripples the trees

Her grave in a row of slabs
is slashed with the sparse dates
of her life: waste, wastage
and the twists of history
with its bundle of 'ifs'

A heap of gifts on the muddy grass:
cards and rain-smudged notes
fragments of poems
her own and others'

An abundance of flowers:
carnations, freesias
heather, foxgloves
a bunch of rowan berries

Pilgrims still pulled
in squally rain to Heptonstall
where from a churchyard's
damp chrysanthemums
comes the humming of her words

LIVING IN BERLIN

used to be a street here / this is where I used to live
old man slumps / lost in wasteground grass

war's gone / but city still has bare patches
bombs under rubble / miserable widowers

cold war begins / no one dies by fire any more
this is the place where / wall will be built

wall splits the city / wall is graffitied
wall is laughing / but enormous

this is where you will live / these are the people who
but what if – / the one I love is –

wall is erected / she plans tunnels
dreams of wings / imagines people on the other side

paces her segment of the city / until
she reaches wall / flaunting itself

time comes when wall / goes out of fashion
is broken down / brick by brick

and then such a seeping and merging of split city
it seems there are fields opening up and it's greener

and more spacious on the new un-walked down
    labyrinth of streets

with their untouched buildings and their different
    smells

in a café she's discovered on the other side
he turns and offers her his pale green wine which she

sips and in his garden there are white poppies
ripe raspberries they eat with buttermilk

in afternoons full of sweet fruit tastes
and in warm evenings they stroll out over city

see wall's space like a tooth gap
explore soft new places with the tongue

A NEW YEAR'S STORY

There was snow under the moonlight
where the train came from

and so to walk at dawn
out into the newly January morning

to be touched on the face
by the warm breath of Louisiana air
is like a gasp of spring

and then to tread a maze of streets
to where the plum-blue sky
thins into rose-pink

and to suddenly come upon
the wide and lapping river
with the sun coming up
beyond the place on the far shore
named Desire

and the clouds becoming colours
like turquoise, like thundery violet
like the pale green of new almonds –

to be here in this daybreak
with the light spilling into
the Mississippi
tinging its quivering ripples
orange, as though little fishes
slithered in the oily water

and to see a steamboat
delicately turn its bulk
peaking tiny waves in its wake –

this, this morning, overwhelms

so that mouths, beestung with tiredness
unable to talk, kiss

while reflections of sunrise
make gold flecks in the iris of an eye

make windows on the waterfront
gleam like brass –

and after this, to find a pink-painted house
with a wrought-iron balcony
where a sign says 'To Let'
and to invent delicious fiction –

that the key is fetched
the room that faces east entered

that a bed offers white linen
lit by this winter sun
fingering through lacy curtains –

but instead to take breakfast
in the café across the road
and to talk of other New Year's mornings

even as the story of this one –

taking place in a southern city
brushed by the waters of the gulf
and washed in a light
that swabs the skin with gold –

unfolding, melts into a new fiction

THE POEM OF THE ALCOHOLIC'S WIFE

Not just the endless empty bottles
the beery taste of kisses;
not just the stench of the bedroom
where his vomit smears the floor;
a cupboard stuffed with secrets
smashed china
photographs ripped from their frames

But, somehow, as well as this
a memory of myself once
in a yellow cotton dress
a breeze off the sea
and his hands gently touching my face;
and of my mother in a corner of the kitchen
writing her journal

and now, a woman who brings me oranges;
a poem thought up in the night
forgotten over breakfast
as the nuzzling child tells of her nightmare
then dragged back by a bunch of lilacs
plucked in the rain
and quickly recorded on a typewriter
balanced on the lap

O'KEEFFE'S SUMMER

I
New York

A cramped country house:
heat clings to the walls like clematis
squabbles explodes through floorboards

This broody family
is an amoeba of relatives
They sprawl around me:
too many screeching children
too many giggly virgins
too many smug mothers

Rooms bulge with them
The library is rank with stale smoke
and nitpicking discussions
The kitchen brims with women
in a mulch of jam-making
The attics echo
with shrill cribbed children

They swelter in the draped parlour
or pace about the lawns
scowling below veiled hats
bickering under spiked parasols

The hefty sky weighs down

In this little basket of landscape
there is nothing but green:
too much dozy green
My eyes in the evenings blur
from gazing at the heady trees

Sometimes a mumble of thunder
trembles the leaves
and a faint rain patters down

The woods close in like clammy hands
The sky is disappearing

II
New Mexico

Here there is a multitude of sky
I pummel it with shouts and loud songs
lie naked under its taut blue sheet
letting the tongue of sun
explore the crevices of skin

Soil is a thin rust-red dust
sprouting only scrub and greyish sagebrush
and scattered with pecked carcasses

I gather up pieces of skeleton
spat out by vultures
I have a home full of found bones
I fondle them: paint and paint
their stark calcium whitenesses

At dusk I stride out
into the breathing desert
The raw hills heave with scarlet
glow in the cinder-light of sunset

I bawl if I want to at the limitless sky
already bruised to dark purples
streaked blood-red by the gashed sun

I kiss the cracked and dazzled ground

I will make icons on canvas
of this bleached landscape
with the infinite wings

LOST

Lost like farthings under the rug:

little black and white photos curled at the edges
a plate hand-painted with tulips
the violet cup, the egg tray
the battered tin scoop in the flour-bin

the names of herbs: their uses
(vervain, coltsfoot, lady's mantle)
a marble slab for pastry
a chopping board of mahogany

the memory of the colour that the wallpaper was
the pattern of stippling on linoleum

The worn, the stroked, the fragile
the particulars of kitchens
all gone in the stripping down, the clearing out
the fitting of units, the modern, the modernisation

Earth sags beneath the weight of dumps and tips
Air's thick with the belch of stoked incinerators

We're greedy for the new, and gobbling fast
Rooms gutted like fish:
the spiky bones of the past scooped out, discarded

The filleted future gleams like silver
Nothing will catch in the throat
Nothing: it will all slip down a treat

PORTRAIT OF ESTELLE, AND AFTER

I

Upstairs in a yellow house sits a woman, motionless
balancing stems of gladioli on her fingers

She recalls colours for the scoop of petals:
cream, pale orange, crimson

There is sunlight on her hands, a smell of oil of
      turpentine
the tinkling of a paintbrush in a jar

He describes the portrait to her as he works:
a glow within the paleness of the flesh tones
bright splashings for the flowers

He explains the use of flecks of colour, rough
      brushstrokes
a dappling of paint to depict light:
techniques he's learning over in France

After the sitting, she stumbles to the door
catching her skirt as she goes on the palette
Paint adheres: a smear of burnt sienna

II

In the cellar of the yellow house
thin black arms plunge again and again into suds

The maid scrubs the blotch
on the pale pink froth of the mistress's dress
In the sticky afternoon sweat gathers at her neck

No wind stirs the dripping silk

III

Trying to remember how her face was once
– eager, full of light, he told her –
she rubs over the canvas cramped fingers

Her bones are stiff with the damp
of this infested, fetid city
where disease has gorged on her children,
where the endlessly shifting price of cotton
has lured her husband from her long ago

She owns nothing now but a portrait
and this yellow house
whose rooms she knows by heart and cannot leave

She walks, creakily, out onto the balcony
where a thin rain touches her face
prickles the taffeta of her frock

The air's steamy as a bath: she gasps for breath
gropes for a breeze that is not there

but grasps a faint sound of mournful jazz
that thickens as a funeral grows near
passes by on the street below her
then moves on towards the graveyard

Later she hears dirges twisted into song
The procession dances back along the road
and she leans out, letting this queer music fall into her
feeling the saxophone sprinkle her spine
get somewhere in behind her dead eyes

IV

They bury Estelle in the graveyard
and hang her portrait in the gallery

Outside the yellow house a huge sign is erected
noting that a famous artist came here once

Across the door is draped a cloth:
the wide brash flag of the USA

Too much music on the streets these days,
they're saying: decent folk can't sleep
Always someone playing jazz: should be regulations

Dolls for sale dressed like slaves and smiling
Sepia reproductions of the quaint old brothels

Strippers dancing in the smoky bars
Black cleaners before sunrise
clearing up the pools of beery vomit

The cemetery stashed with plastic flowers
The damp sky white as marble

Bandages bind the fingers tight
Blindfolds wrap the open eyes
Rags stuff the mouths of saxophones

V

The mute begin to peel away their dressings
to thud out warnings loud as drumbeats

After the tear gas and police have failed
bullets will be the only way to silence them

A stink of burning: naked flagpoles
Scraps of charred cloth scattering the lawns

The swelling delta gulps at the city
Mud encroaches on the lime-tree streets

In the squelchy graveyard, flesh falls away
Bones float out on slick towards the sea

Out of the drowning gallery washes a ghostly
      painting
Its eyes are seeing: light, light, light

The swamp rises, crushing its irises
The river edges crumble away

Behind a ripped flag, a yellow door is visible
and black hands turning a key in a lock

Descendants of a washerwoman
shelter in an upstairs room
that has a whiff of turps about it

Above them in the empty attic they can hear
faint bird sounds, footsteps

and through the thicket of the rain
a saxophone

THESE SANDS, THIS SHORE

We have walked these sands so many times together

We have walked them every time I visit you
here at the rim of the city
in a place that feels like an old stone
worn smooth and rounded by its closeness to the sea:

the nestled houses   paintwork faded by salt air
blown sand sifted   on the pavements
the slaty roofs   the smoke plumes rising
the haberdashers   and the shabby cafés

It's grown familiar as our friendship
this shoreline where we walk together
telling one another all the details of our lives:
things that we tell to no one else
things that will ease with the telling
with the walking on sand   the soft inrushes of sea

To feel   on an afternoon of sadness
a lifting   a lightening
with the filtering   of fine sand
sun-warmed   through my fingers
and the finding of the pearled whelk shell

or to feel the clenched mind   rammed with guilt
unfurl in the new light   of a spring evening

or just to let my tired feet be soothed
by water   and the rub of cool sand

We have walked these sands in silence
gathering shells   fragments of old china
We have paddled   clambered breakwaters
walked until we've reached the black rocks
where the blue mussels crunch beneath our feet
then turned   and with the sea at the other shoulder
walked back   towards your home

where the beach creeps in   with shells
bits of smoothed blue-patterned china
seagull feathers   footprints of sand

where once there were lilies in a white vase
and once narcissus   scenting all the rooms

where we have feasted like Greeks on ripe olives
eaten herbs from the back green
or drunk   on wintry evenings   bowls of thick soup
against the cold of rattling gales
that spatter the window panes with salt

We have looked out at the bluish waves
pulled up to the sea wall by a full moon
and seen the lights strung out along the coast
the blink of lighthouse from the island where the
        seabirds dwell

I have slept beneath embroidered sheets
with sea sounds faint at the window
woken in the morning to a haar upon the water
and you   in cherry coloured satin   making tea

Here   where the past is not smothered   but breathes
the heart grows softer   being washed like a shell
by the lapping sea   the grains of sand
and your presence   wind-gentle

We have walked these sands so many times together
and I have found myself healed   here on this beach
your words   your coat   your arms around me
closely